OWJC

GREAT WHITE SHARKS

The Amazing World of Sharks

GREAT WHITE SHRKS

By Elizabeth Roseborough

MASON CREST

Mason Crest
450 Parkway Drive, Suite D
Broomall, Pennsylvania 19008
(866) MCP-BOOK (toll-free)
www.masoncrest.com

First printing
9 8 7 6 5 4 3 2 1
Printed in the USA

ISBN (hardback) 978-1-4222-4126-4
ISBN (series) 978-1-4222-4121-9
ISBN (ebook) 978-1-4222-7675-4

Library of Congress Cataloging-in-Publication Data

Names: Roseborough, Elizabeth, author.
Title: Great white sharks / Elizabeth Roseborough.
Description: Broomall, Pennsylvania: Mason Crest, [2019] | Series: The amazing world of sharks | Includes bibliographical references and index.
Identifiers: LCCN 2018013889 (print) | LCCN 2018018312 (ebook) | ISBN 9781422276754 (eBook) | ISBN 9781422241264 (hardback) | ISBN 9781422241219 (series)
Subjects: LCSH: White shark--Juvenile literature. | White shark--Behavior--Juvenile literature.
Classification: LCC QL638.95.L3 (ebook) | LCC QL638.95.L3 R67 2019 (print) | DDC 597.3/3--dc23
LC record available at https://lccn.loc.gov/2018013889

Developed and Produced by National Highlights Inc.
Editor: Keri De Deo
Interior and cover design: Priceless Digital Media
Production: Michelle Luke

CONTENTS

KEY ICONS TO LOOK FOR:

 Words to Understand: These words with their easy-to-understand definitions will increase the reader's understanding of the text while building vocabulary skills.

 Sidebars: This boxed material within the main text allows readers to build knowledge, gain insights, explore possibilities, and broaden their perspectives by weaving together additional information to provide realistic and holistic perspectives.

 Educational Videos: Readers can view videos by scanning our QR codes, providing them with additional educational content to supplement the text. Examples include news coverage, moments in history, speeches, iconic sports moments, and much more!

 Text-Dependent Questions: These questions send the reader back to the text for more careful attention to the evidence presented there.

 Research Projects: Readers are pointed toward areas of further inquiry connected to each chapter. Suggestions are provided for projects that encourage deeper research and analysis.

 Series Glossary of Key Terms: This back-of-the book glossary contains terminology used throughout this series. Words found here increase the reader's ability to read and comprehend higher-level books and articles in this field.

FUN FACTS...
GETTING TO KNOW THEM

TIGER SHARK
Named for the vertical striped markings along its body, but they fade with age.

MAKO SHARK
Known as the race car of sharks for its fast swimming speed!

BULL SHARK
Named for its stocky shape, broad, flat snout, and aggressive, unpredictable behavior!

RAYS
Rays and sharks belong to the same family. A ray is basically a flattened shark.

GREAT WHITE SHARK

With jaws this fierce, they don't call it "Great" for nothing!

BLUE SHARK

Known by their distinct blue and white coloring, their large eyes, and long snout.

HAMMERHEAD SHARK

Yes, those are eyes mounted on the side of its head, giving it 360-degree vision!

THE

Th
its
s

WORDS TO UNDERSTAND:

habitat: The home or natural environment of an animal, person, or plant.

marine biologist: A scientist who studies the plant and animal life of the ocean.

predator: An animal that hunts other living things.

prey: An animal that is hunted by other animals.

satellite tag: A special device marine biologists place on marine animals that allows the animals' movements to be tracked. This device sends signals to a satellite in space. The satellite then returns the messages to a computer monitored by marine biologists. This allows the scientists to learn valuable information about the animals' habits.

RESHER SHARK
is clever shark uses
unique long tail fin to
tun and catch prey!

CHAPTER 1

INTRODUCING GREAT WHITES

Picture it. It's a hot summer day and you're vacationing at the beach with your family. The sun is shining, not a cloud in the sky, and you're swimming in the ocean, having a fun time with your friends. You're laughing and joking, and then you go silent: you can feel your heart pounding as you see a large gray fin pop up from between the waves. You scream, "SHARK!" and panic ensues. Your heart beats fast. You and your friends frantically swim to the shore as fast as you can, and then breathlessly you look back at the sea, thankful that you survived an encounter with one of nature's most-feared creatures—the great white shark.

Few ocean animals strike fear into the hearts of swimmers, divers, and fishermen quite like the great white shark.

Great white sharks rarely attack unprovoked.

We've all heard of great white sharks before—the very idea that one of these majestic, terrifying animals could be swimming near a beach is enough to send people home for the day. While great whites rarely attack unless provoked, they're known for frequenting coastal areas, making the scary sightings common. Even though most people will never encounter a great white shark in their lifetime, it's important to remember that the moment we step into the ocean, we're leaving our **habitat** and entering that of the great white shark.

LEARNING ABOUT GREAT WHITE SHARKS

It's not always easy for **marine biologists** to study great white sharks. Getting too close to these giant creatures can be dangerous, especially if the shark feels surrounded or threatened by the scientists trying to study them. While they rarely attack unless provoked, one large bite from a great white shark can be fatal. Even cage diving (when scientists wear wet suits and submerg themselves underwater in a strong metal cage to observe ocean life) can be a bad idea. Great white sharks have been known to use their powerful bodies to enter the cages, putting scientists in danger. Marine biologists have not given up on studying great white sharks, but they have had to get creative to learn more about these fantastic animals.

One way that scientists are learning more about great white sharks is through satellite tracking. In 2013, marine biologists placed a **satellite tag** on a 14.5 ft. (4.4 m) long female great white shark they named Lydia. This tag allowed the biologists to track Lydia's movements over time. The tag sends a signal to a satellite in space, and that signal comes back to a computer monitored by a scientist. These signals show Lydia's movements on a map, providing information on her travels over time. As it turns out, great white sharks are fantastic swimmers. They put Michael Phelps to shame. Lydia has actually swum across the Atlantic Ocean, from the eastern shores of the United States, past the islands of Bermuda, finally reaching the United Kingdom. Lydia is the first shark known to be able to swim this distance. Marine biologists aren't sure why Lydia swims so far, but they're going to keep studying her movements to find out. She is also a champion diver—she has dived more than 4,000 ft. (1219 m) under water! To track Lydia, visit her profile page at http://www.ocearch.org/profile/lydia/.

CHOMP- SHARK ATTACK!

Just like people, great white sharks have places where they like to hang out. One of these places is called the "Red Triangle." The Red Triangle is an area off the coast of California in which many people enjoy surfing and swimming. The area is known for having a high number of great white shark attacks. Thirty-eight percent of all the attacks that occur in the United States occur in the Red Triangle area. Great white sharks do not come to this area looking for people, however.

Marine biologists capture and tag great white sharks to learn more about how to protect them.

They come to this area looking for one of their favorite foods: seals. While great white sharks certainly prefer to eat seals over attacking people, occasionally, attacks do happen, both on people and on their belongings. In April of 2017, a kayaker named Brian Correiar was enjoying the California waters and learned this lesson all too well. As he was kayaking through the quiet ocean water, he heard a loud bang, and the next thing he knew, he was in the water, no longer in his kayak. Just 3 ft. (.9 m) away, he saw a great white shark chomping on his boat! Luckily, the shark decided it was more interested in eating the kayak than eating Brian, who escaped unscathed. This type of "attack" is fairly common. Often, great white sharks will become curious about people and their belongings, sneak up on them silently, take a bite of their boat or surfboard, and then slowly sink away, without hurting the people.

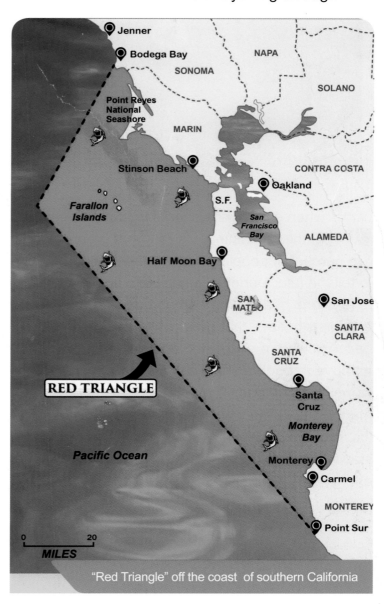

"Red Triangle" off the coast of southern California

Curious about Brian's view as a great white chomped his kayak? Check out this video to see what it's like to come face to face with a great white shark!

Often, when great white sharks ____ually do get a bite of a person, they don't like what they're tasting. It's rar___ hat great white shark bites are fatal. Eighty-five percent of people who have been bitten by a great white shark have lived to tell the tale. During a great white shark attack, it's common for the shark to take one bite of a person and decide that it is no longer interested. Marine biologists believe that great white sharks do not enjoy preying on people because we are simply too bony for their tastes! Bones take a long time to move through a shark's digestive system, which stops them from eating some kinds of food. They prefer the fatty blubber they find on seals and other marine life. Great white sharks are huge animals; they can weigh up to 2,400 lbs. (1088.622 kg). It takes an enormous number of calories for their bodies to stay warm and keep moving, and fatty ocean animals provide them with the energy they need.

Great whites prefer eating seals rather than humans.

SHARK MYTH: GREAT WHITE SHARKS WANT TO EAT PEOPLE.

FALSE! Great white sharks think of people the way that many people think of broccoli: they'll eat it if they're super hungry and there isn't much else around, but it's definitely not their first choice. When great whites injure people, it's usually because they're in the way of a shark getting to their prey or because the shark feels threatened by the person. Great white sharks do not go out of their way to attack people. If they're left alone, it's rare that they'll attack. There are many tales of great white sharks biting people and then swimming away after they get a taste. We simply are not a great white shark's preferred dinner.

TEXT-DEPENDENT QUESTIONS:

1. Why do scientists think that great white sharks prefer not to eat people?

2. How do marine biologists track Lydia?

3. Where is the Red Triangle?

 RESEARCH PROJECT:

Scientists are working hard to protect people from great white shark attacks. Research the types of technology currently being used to prevent shark attacks.

WORDS TO UNDERSTAND:

captivity: Animals living in captivity live under human care, either as pets, in zoos, or in aquariums.

hypothesis: A possible answer to a scientific question based on research.

pinniped: A species of fin-footed marine mammals, including seals, otters, and walruses. These animals live in shallow coastal waters.

temperate: A moderate temperature—not too hot, not too cold.

warm-blooded: A warm-blooded animal is able to control its own body temperature using its metabolism, as opposed to cold-blooded animals who must rely on the environment to control their body temperatures. Warm-blooded animals are also called endotherms.

CHAPTER 2

HABITAT OF THE GREAT WHITE SHARK

From California to New Zealand to South Africa, great white sharks can be found in many places throughout the world. The habitat of the great white shark is a topic that scientists have studied extensively. It's important for people to know where great whites like to hunt, breed, and socialize for a number of reasons. First, scientists want to know where they can find great whites so that they're able to study and track them. For many years, great white sharks have been hard to study due to their dangerous nature, and many biologists want to learn as much as they can about these giant predators. Since great white sharks are unable to be held in **captivity**, marine biologists must study them in their natural habitat. Secondly, people need to know where great whites live so that they know not to surf or swim in those waters! Until recently, great white sharks have been difficult to track. In this

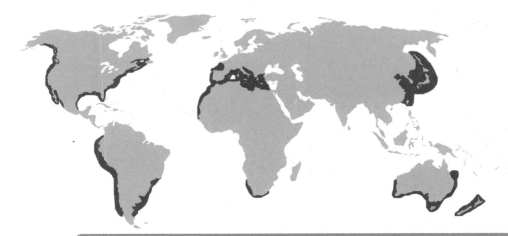

The great white shark inhabits several coastlines across the globe.

chapter, we'll talk about how great white sharks choose their habitat, where they live, how scientists track great whites, and why the population of great white sharks is on the rise.

There are many unique facts about the great white shark that affect its habitat choice, and one of those is the fact that they are **warm-blooded** (endothermic) animals. This means that they have the ability to regulate their own body temperature, just like people, cats, and dogs. Rather than staying at a toasty 98.6°F (37°C) like humans, great white sharks strive to maintain a body temperature of 79°F (26°C), regardless of the temperature of the water around them. Sharks heat up when they increase physical activity (just like you do when you exercise), and they cool down when they rest. It's important that great whites have this ability, as they often need to use short bursts of energy (like a sprinter running a race) to stun and attack their prey. The ability to heat up and cool down allows their bodies to adjust

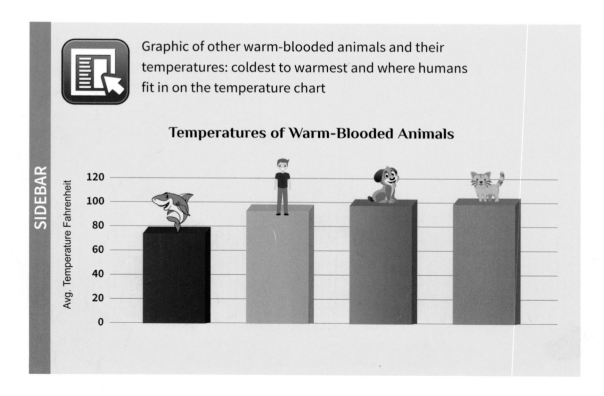

Graphic of other warm-blooded animals and their temperatures: coldest to warmest and where humans fit in on the temperature chart

Temperatures of Warm-Blooded Animals

to any water temperature, which is essential if a great white needs to follow its food source into cold or warm waters. Most sharks are cold-blooded, so the fact that the great white shark is warm-blooded makes them special. Most great white sharks tend to make their habitat in waters that range from 54°F–75°F (12.22°C–23.89°C), but they have no trouble swimming through colder or warmer waters from time to time.

Many great white sharks prefer to live in coastal areas, allowing them easy access to their favorite foods: animals known as **pinnipeds**. Pinnipeds spend time on land and in water, and great whites often lurk near the coast waiting for pinnipeds to start their underwater hunting sessions. Since great whites prefer **temperate** waters, they are often found above and below the equator. They rarely enter tropical waters, such as those in the Caribbean. When great whites are actively hunting, their body temperatures rise quickly, and even with the ability to control their body temperatures, the warm temperatures of tropical waters can make it difficult for them to cool down

Although some sharks survive in captivity, great whites rarely do.

quickly (just like if you were to exercise and then had to sit outside in the hot sun—your body would have trouble cooling down, even if you were sweating and drinking water). It's also rare that great white sharks will live in polar or arctic waters. The cold temperatures are simply too uncomfortable, even though there is a large amount of prey for them to eat.

Great whites tend to live either in coastal waters or in deep, deep ocean waters, far from the coast but rarely in-between. They are either resting on the bottom of the ocean or swimming near the surface to hunt. Great white sharks have been recorded resting as deep in the ocean as 820 ft. (250 m). It's hard for scientists to study great whites when they're deep underwater, but recent tracking devices are helping us to learn more about what happens when they disappear into the dark abyss of the deep sea.

HOW DO MARINE BIOLOGISTS TRACK GREAT WHITE SHARKS WHEN THEY CAN'T SEE THEM?

For a long time, all of the information we knew about great whites came from what we could see. We didn't know much about what happened when they left coastlines or swam to deep waters. Scientists are working hard to learn as much as they can about great white sharks, and they have four main techniques they use to track these giants. The first type of tracker is called a PAT tag. This tracker consists of sensors for light, depth, and temperature, but it does not transmit the shark's location. This sensor is good for telling us what conditions sharks prefer. The second type of tracker is a SPOT tag. The SPOT tag has a transmitter that sends the shark's location to a satellite each time the shark comes to the surface of the water, helping us learn more about where in the world great whites tend to prefer to spend their time. The third type of tracker is an acoustic tag—this is implanted in the shark's body and sends ultrasonic pings to receivers on the ocean floor, allowing scientists to track the shark each time he or she comes within 900 ft. (274 m) of the receiver. These are often utilized in great white shark hot spots. The last—and newest—type of shark tracker is called a Smart Tag. A Smart Tag is like a GoPro camera for sharks. The tag attaches to the shark's fin and transmits everything the shark sees and hears back to scientists. This helps us learn about how great white sharks hunt, interact with each other, and travel from habitat to habitat. This technology is expensive—sharks can swim with up to $10,000 worth of technology on their bodies!

When we think of great whites, many of us picture what we see in movies: huge gray or white animals swimming barely under the waves, showing their pointy fins as a warning sign to get out of the way quickly before they attack. While we often think of great white sharks swimming close to the surface, this is not always the case. For a large part of their lives, sharks live toward the bottom of the ocean, waiting to strike their prey. They lurk under the cover of dark water, allowing them to become nearly invisible to their prey above. Their excellent eyesight, even in the dark, makes it easy for them to keep an eye on potential prey while hiding in the shadows.

When it's time to hunt, sharks are able to propel their body weight toward the surface at a speed of up to 25 mph (40 kmph), grasping their prey in their jaws without a fight. Shallow water is essential for sharks to be able to rest on the ocean floor while also stalking their prey.

Scientists are working hard to figure out why some sharks seem to prefer living near the coast, and others prefer to live in deep ocean water, but thus far, they have not been able to pinpoint what causes sharks to prefer different areas. Scientists also are not sure why some sharks seem to switch between living in coastal waters and living in deep water, even when food sources are readily available in coastal waters. Next, we'll discuss the areas of the world where the majority of great white sharks choose to call home. There are a number of **hypotheses** as to why great whites choose these areas.

CALIFORNIA

There are many locations along the California coastline that marine biologists refer to as "hot spots" for great white sharks. Through tracking, these spots have been identified as places that great white sharks visit with high frequency. There are a few different hypotheses as to why great whites are inclined to repeatedly visit these locations. First, these areas tend to be warmer than the surrounding ocean. Due to the shallow water, the sun is able to heat the water quickly. Scientists are unsure as to why warm-blooded sharks appear to prefer warm water, especially since they seem to overheat in tropical locations. It's hypothesized that a great white's enjoyment of warm, shallow water may be similar to how cats enjoy the feeling of lying in the sun. Secondly, these California hot spots are full of seals and sting rays, both of which great whites hunt frequently. It's hard to imagine that the great white shark could fall prey to another predator, but it does happen. Orca whales (also known as killer whales) sometimes come together as a group to hunt great whites, and shallow California coastal waters tend to be free of orcas, allowing the sharks to hunt safely without having to be on alert for danger. Many scientists used to believe

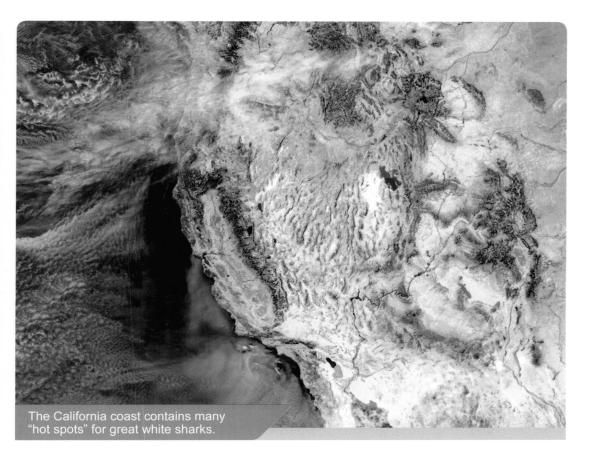

The California coast contains many "hot spots" for great white sharks.

that great white sharks were common in the Pacific Northwest area of the United States, but current studies show that great whites actually prefer to make their home in the more temperate waters of the Southern California coastline.

SOUTH AFRICA

The southernmost point of South Africa is known as a hotbed for great white shark activity. An island near the South African coast—Dyer Island—is especially known for great white shark sightings. Some great white sharks migrate seasonally between South Africa and the western coast of Australia—a distance of nearly 7,000 mi (11,265 km) Locals say that if you visit southern South Africa, there is a 99 percent chance that you will get

Great white sharks have been sighted around Dyer Island off the coast of South Africa.

to see a great white shark. Great whites often prey on a pinniped known as the Cape fur seal in this area. Sadly, the great white shark population is diminishing slowly in South Africa. Scientists are not completely sure of the reason, but a high population of orca whales may be the culprit.

SOUTHERN ALASKA

Recently, tracking devices have alerted biologists that great white sharks are venturing out of their water temperature comfort zone to live and hunt in the waters off the coasts of southeast Alaska. It's likely that they migrate from the more comfortable waters of southern California to hunt the plentiful, fatty marine mammals that are abundant on the shores of Alaska. It's unlikely that great whites live near Alaska long term, but as long as seals stay plentiful in the area, sightings of great whites are likely to continue. Like many of the great white shark's activities, the full reason behind this migration is yet to be discovered.

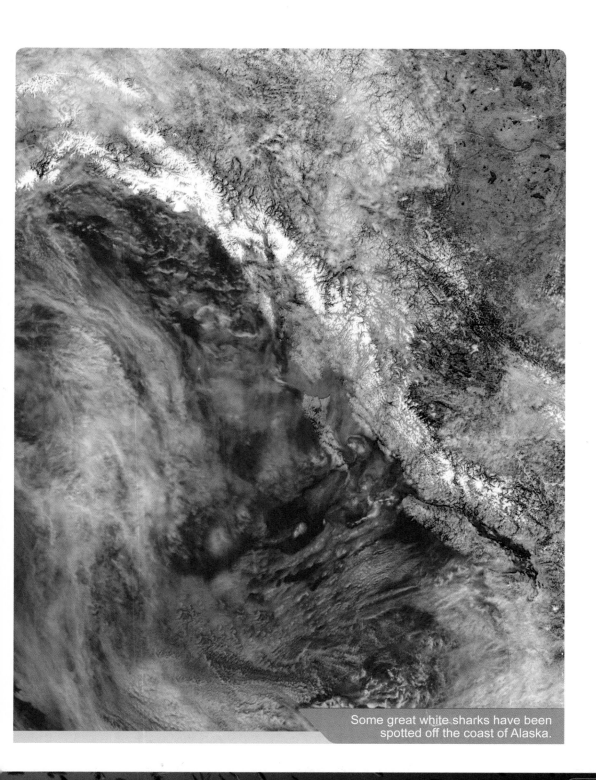

Some great white sharks have been spotted off the coast of Alaska.

NEW ZEALAND

Great white sharks surround the islands of New Zealand, and residents of the area are used to doing their best to live in harmony with these potentially dangerous fish. In this area, younger great whites tend to stick to the rocky coast, but young and full-grown adults live in both coastal areas and the open ocean surrounding the island. Satellite tagging has shown that many sharks migrate between New Zealand, Australia, and South Africa. While living so close to sharks can be scary for New Zealanders, great whites are important for controlling the populations of various animals on the island. The New Zealand government has many measures in place to protect great whites.

New Zealand provides a protective environment for great white sharks.

FLORIDA

The majority of shark bites and attacks that occur in the world happen in the United States off the coast of Florida. Marine biologists believe that Florida's temperate waters attract great whites that typically live in the waters of the Atlantic Ocean on the northeast coast of the United States during the frigid winter months. Great white sharks that swim south in the winters tend to go back and forth between Florida and the Carolinas. While living in the southeast coastal waters, sharks usually stay in fairly shallow areas looking for prey. During the warmer summer months, great whites tend to migrate back to their New England home where the water temperature is cooler and more suitable for their needs.

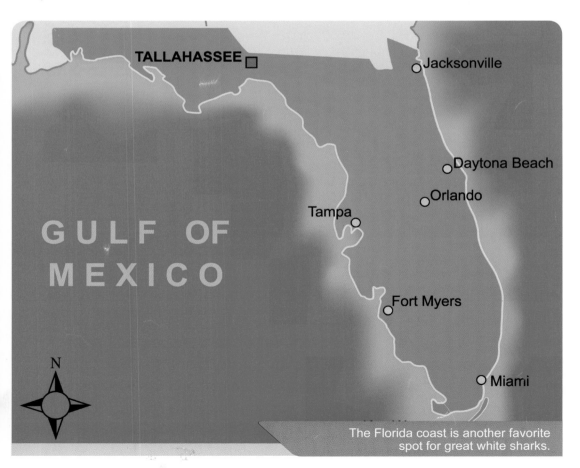

The Florida coast is another favorite spot for great white sharks.

GREAT WHITE SHARK POPULATION

Marine biologists are working hard to determine how many great white sharks are left in the wild, but due to their elusive nature, it's impossible to get an exact number. Scientists estimate that there are approximately thirty-five hundred great white sharks remaining in the wild. This makes great whites a vulnerable species. Vulnerable is the level below endangered. While great white sharks still need to be protected, there are many things being done to ensure that their population increases.

Get a shark's perspective of the ocean from this National Geographic video.

UNITED STATES GREAT WHITE SHARK POPULATION ON THE RISE

While it's sad to imagine, some people enjoy hunting great white sharks for sport. These majestic animals tend to put up a serious fight when they're caught, and some people like the thrill of being so close to danger, even though it means they are harming an animal and likely taking its life. Unfortunately, great white shark hunting caused a serious population decline in the 1960s and 1970s. Often, the sharks that were caught were either stuffed and used as trophies or sold solely for their teeth and fins.

Great white sharks were once hunted for their teeth and fins.

In the past twenty years, many government organizations have made it illegal to hunt great white sharks, and as a result, scientists believe that their population has been steadily increasing.

SIDEBAR

HOW YOU CAN HELP PROTECT GREAT WHITE SHARKS

Learning and teaching others about the importance of great white sharks is a great first step in protecting these creatures from human harm. When people understand that great white sharks are not out to hurt people, they're less likely to engage in harmful behavior. If you're interested in looking at great white shark jaws and teeth, look at them at a museum. Don't buy them from a gift shop when you take a vacation to the beach. In the unlikely event that the teeth and jaws are real, it's likely that a shark was killed so that someone could make money off of selling their body parts. Donating to organizations that protect great white sharks is another option for helping scientists learn more about these creatures and how to protect them from harm.

TEXT-DEPENDENT QUESTIONS:

1. The great white shark population is decreasing in South Africa. Why?

2. Where is the population of great white sharks growing?

3. Why do many great white sharks prefer to live in shallow coastal waters?

RESEARCH PROJECT:

While the population of the great white shark is on the rise in the United States, the same is not true of the great white shark population in Chile. Research what caused the great white shark population to decline in Chile, and come up with ideas that could help the population begin to grow again.

WORDS TO UNDERSTAND:

apex predator: A hunting animal at the top of its ecosystem's food chain.

breaching: A behavior in which ocean animals use tremendous speed to propel their entire bodies out of the water and into the air. Predatory marine animals often breach while catching their prey.

pup: A baby shark.

CHAPTER 3

THE GREAT WHITE'S DIET, BEHAVIOR, AND BIOLOGY

In many ways, the great white shark is still a creature of mystery! Marine biologists are just beginning to truly understand the diet, behavior, and biology of great whites. Due to their dangerous nature, it's been difficult to study great whites, but scientists are learning more about them every day through tracking and observation. In this chapter, we'll talk about what great whites like (and don't like) to eat, how they hunt, how they interact with one another, and their physical biology (how their bodies work).

Great white sharks help keep the ocean balanced.

DIET

The great white shark is an **apex predator** in the marine food chain. Not many sea animals are able to challenge a great white (there are a few animals who will attack a great white, such as a group of orca whales, but this is a rare occurrence). A great white

Great white sharks help keep the seal population down, which helps balance the ecosystem.

shark's diet is an important part of keeping ocean ecosystems in balance. Without great white sharks, the ocean would not be able to support the exploding populations of animals that usually fall prey to sharks.

While great whites seem to prefer pinnipeds, such as seals, otters, and sea lions, they are not known to be picky eaters. They'll eat fish, smaller sharks, and even sea birds! Interestingly, it seems that older great whites will sometimes prey on younger great whites; no one is quite sure why this occurs. Great whites have been observed **breaching** to catch birds. Great white shark **pups** do not have jaws that are mature enough to attack large marine animals, and their diets mainly consist of small fish until they

A young great white's jaws are underdeveloped for large prey.

A curious or defensive great white will take a bite out of a surfboard, but it doesn't mean they have bad eyesight.

grow large and strong enough to prey on pinnipeds and larger fish. Their diets will begin to change once they begin to mature and reach about 12 ft. (3.7 m) in length.

Like many humans, if given the choice between a meal high in protein and a meal high in fat, a great white shark will always choose the meal high in fat. The fat found in large sea mammals gives great whites the energy they need to propel their bodies through the ocean, find mates, and hunt for their prey. Great white sharks tend to

Great White Shark vs. Human Diet

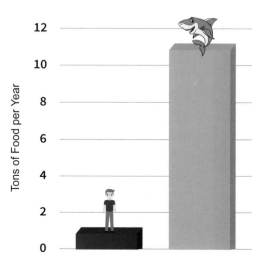

consume about 11 tons (6.35 metric tons) of food per year. For comparison's sake, the average 150-lb. (68 kg) human consumes about 1,000 lbs. (454 kg) of food each year. While great white sharks prefer to hunt every two days, they are capable of going months between feedings if food is scarce.

Great whites are able to adapt their diets to their environments. For example, a great white shark that lives in the northeastern United States during warm months does not have the option to feast on pinnipeds and is more likely to

SHARK MYTH: SHARKS HAVE POOR EYESIGHT, WHICH CAUSES THEM TO MISTAKE SURFERS FOR SEALS.

Nothing could be further from the truth—sharks have excellent eyesight! If a shark takes a bite of a surfer, there are a few possible reasons behind the attack. One reason is that sharks are extremely curious. If the great white has never encountered surfers before, it may truly want to know what they taste like, and it will likely swim away after it discovers that humans are more bone than fat. It's also possible that a shark feels threatened and is trying to defend itself. Lastly, it's also possible that the shark could be starving. When a great white is extremely hungry, it will eat something it doesn't like. Make no mistake—a shark knows exactly what it's attacking long before it takes the first chomp.

Great white sharks are not necessarily picky eaters.

fill up on large fish (including small sharks and whales) and sea birds. While great white sharks do certainly prefer to eat fatty sea animals, they have been known to take bites of other things, either out of desperation or curiosity. Many shark attacks consist of great white sharks taking a bite out of a human, deciding humans are too bony for their tastes, and then moving on to look for something else. Great whites are also known to take bites out of surfboards and paddleboards, likely just to find out what these things are.

SIDEBAR

HOW DO SHARKS LEARN TO HUNT?

Research has shown that great white sharks are able to learn information. Older sharks (who are less athletic than younger sharks) tend to have a higher success rate when hunting seals than younger, more able-bodied great whites. This shows that hunting is not simply a matter of athletic ability, and that it takes time to learn the best hunting techniques. Some sharks have even learned how to recover from hunting mistakes. Most sharks will give up after a seal escapes, but some sharks have been observed "trying again" successfully after a first failed hunting attempt.

Watch a seal take on a great white shark.

This great white breached the water off the coast of South Africa.

BEHAVIOR – HUNTING

Great white sharks are extremely curious animals, and they have exceptional ears, noses, and eyes to help them locate and attack their prey. Hunting is an art for sharks—they have several techniques that they use depending on the situation, and they learn how to get better at hunting as they grow older.

There are three main methods that great white sharks use to hunt. The most common hunting method is to surprise their prey from the bottom of the ocean, where the dark gray color of the top of the shark's body blends in with the rocks below, making it difficult for their prey to spot them when looking down from above. This is called the underwater approach. The shark will lurk at the bottom of the ocean, looking upward until they find the prey they'd like to attack, and then they propel their body toward the surface, sneaking up on their prey from beneath. This quick approach serves two purposes: it allows the shark to bite and stun its prey at the same time. Often, this is when great white sharks are sighted by humans. The shark breaches out of the water, sometimes lifting its entire body into the air with the prey in its mouth.

The next most common hunting method used by great white sharks is the surface-charge approach. The shark will swim at the surface of the water, sprint-swimming toward its prey. Before surface charging, the great white sometimes spy-hops its prey—meaning it peeks above the surface of the water to get a better look at where it's going to strike. This is the type of

DO GREAT WHITE SHARKS GET SCARED WHEN THEY HUNT?

Surprise: yes! It may shock you to learn that the vicious great white shark does get nervous about getting hurt while hunting. Before striking its prey, a great white's eyes will roll back in its head to provide protection from injury. Many great white sharks have been observed with scars around their eyes from the sharp teeth and claws of pinnipeds that chose to fight back by going after the shark's eyes. Often, great whites will take a first bite out of their prey and then lurk nearby while the prey bleeds to death, rather than fighting with the animal they've attacked. Just like rolling their eyes back in their heads, this allows sharks to protect themselves from the sharp claws and teeth of their prey. Seals are known to put up an especially tough fight to a great white, often leading to injuries for the shark. Sometimes, after taking the first bite, sharks swim away without eating the animal they have attacked. It's likely that sharks do this either because they do not like the taste of their prey, or they have realized that the prey's body is not fatty enough to meet their nutritional needs.

attack we often see in movies: the shark's fin is sticking out of the top of the water. Great whites are fast swimmers, so this method is often successful, but it does give the prey a chance of spotting the fin and escaping.

A shark fin terrifies most observers.

The least common method of hunting for great whites is upside down swimming, known as the inverted approach. The shark will roll over, hiding its fin under the surface of the water, and swim upside down to sneak attack its prey. This method takes a lot of energy, as it's difficult (and likely uncomfortable) for a shark to swim upside down.

Great whites will swim upside down to catch their prey.

BEHAVIOR – SOCIAL

Great whites are extremely intelligent creatures with brains that can reach up to 2 ft. (.61 m) in length. While they are social with each other, great whites are also known to pop their heads out of the water near boats to check out the people on board. They'll look each person in the eye, seemingly to get a feel for the person, and then move on to someone new. The fact that they're able to hunt large pinnipeds is also a sign of their intelligence; seals are some of the smartest creatures in the ocean, and outsmarting them (especially when they are in a group setting) requires some savvy trickery.

Great white sharks are curious creatures.

Great white sharks have been observed seemingly "playing" with sea birds—grabbing the bird gently in their jaws, swimming with the bird (keeping its head above the surface), and then releasing it unharmed. They've also been observed "playing" with human divers in a similar way—lightly grabbing them

Although we know a lot about great whites, there's still much to learn.

by the hand, taking them on some twirls through the water, and letting them go without hurting them. Great whites seem to be curious and inquisitive creatures, using all of their senses to learn more about the world around them, especially when something new (such as a boat with people on board) enters their environment.

Biologists used to believe that great white sharks were solitary animals, but new research shows that they are actually quite social. While great whites do tend to hunt alone, it seems that great whites have a social hierarchy, and tend to travel in groups. Just like humans, great whites seem to have friends, and dominance within friend groups is based on gender and size. Female sharks have a higher social standing than male sharks, and the bigger shark is the shark in charge. Great whites tend to avoid confrontation, and a fight between sharks is rare (when fights do happen, they're typically due to one shark trying to steal another shark's food). Just like you, all great whites have a personality: some are outgoing, some are aggressive, some are timid, some are playful, and no two are the same.

Great whites appear to seasonally migrate in groups. When seals leave an area, great whites tend to leave the area as well. While migration often occurs because the sharks are following a food source, sometimes the reason for the migration is unknown. Recently, biologists tracked a large group of great whites that migrated to an area in-between California and Hawaii, and the scientists are still unsure as to why this migration happened. These mystery migrations happen frequently, and it's possible that this is when mating occurs. Little is known about the mating behavior of great whites.

Tracking has shown that some great whites seem to have very close bonds with each other. They'll swim together and occasionally even hunt together.

Great whites do not always travel alone. This pair was spotted outside Neptune Islands in South Australia.

It's unclear how sharks decide which sharks they'd like to be friends with, but it's clear that great white "cliques" do exist. Sometimes, great whites will share their prey with their friends or with smaller sharks.

BIOLOGY

Great white sharks were around before dinosaurs, and there are many aspects of their biological makeup that have helped them to remain an apex predator for over 400 million years.

BODY SHAPE

A great white shark gets its name from the color of its belly, as the top (dorsal) half of the shark ranges from light to dark gray. Their pointy, torpedo-like body shape allows them to propel through the water with incredible speed and accuracy, and their pointy faces give great whites a built-in mechanism with which to stun their prey.

Great white sharks are specifically designed for speed.

BRAIN

As previously mentioned, great white sharks have enormous brains that can reach up to 24 in. (61 cm) in length. This large brain size makes sense. A great white is constantly processing sensory information.

NOSE

While a great white shark has many senses that make it a top predator, the sense of smell comes out on top. Their sense of smell is so precise that they can detect one drop of blood in ten billion drops of water. The great white's nostrils are located on the underside of its snout just above its mouth.

Great whites have a keen sense of smell.

EYES

Great white sharks have excellent eyesight, both above and under water, and they are easily able to switch between the two. The retina of a great white's eye is divided into two sections. One section is used for day vision, and the other is used for night vision. The ability to blend in with the ocean floor

The great white's eyes have a protective layer

while seeing perfectly at night is one of the many reasons that great whites can easily sneak up on their prey.

EARS

When looking at a picture of a great white, it's tough to spot its external ears. Their ears are located behind their eyes, and they look nothing like human ears—they're simply very small openings. These ears are small but strong, as they allow sharks to pick up on tiny vibrations in the water around them that human ears could never

The great white's ears are a slight hole behind the eye.

detect. Their ears also have an interesting feature called an ear stone. This is a tiny rock-like organ that moves with gravity, allowing sharks to understand their position in the water (moving up, moving down, right-side-up, or upside down), an important ability to have while hunting prey.

JAWS

Great whites are known for their teeth for good reason. The average full-grown great white has up to three thousand teeth! Their teeth can be up to 3 in. (7.62 cm) long and are formed in up to seven rows, and they allow them to kill their prey with a single bite. The interior rows of teeth are able to retract into the shark's mouth, just like a cat's claws can retract into its paws. Much like humans, great whites have teeth of many shapes and sizes. Some teeth are for tearing and some are for piercing, but none are for chewing. Great whites do not chew their food. They prefer to tear off pieces of flesh to swallow whole.

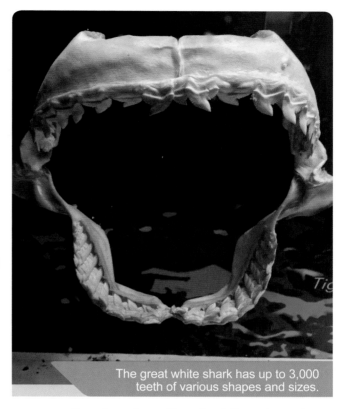

The great white shark has up to 3,000 teeth of various shapes and sizes.

FINS

In the movies, the telltale sign of an impending shark attack is a gray fin sticking out of the water. This fin on the top of the shark's body is called the dorsal fin, and it's used to help the shark stabilize its body as it swims through the water. The pectoral fins look a bit like arms, as they are attached to the underside of the shark's body and are used to help propel the great white through the water (just like you would use your arms to swim). Great whites have incredible control over their pectoral fins, allowing them to attack prey with great accuracy. The caudal fin is what makes up the shark's tail. Most species of sharks have caudal fins that are much bigger on the top than on the bottom, but great whites are different—their caudal fin is nearly

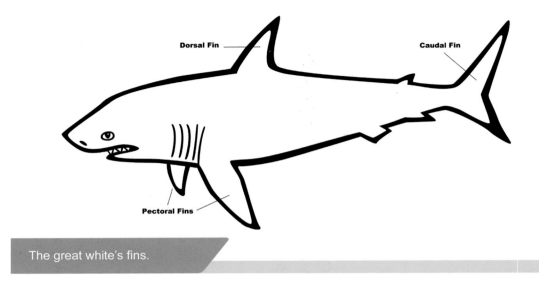

The great white's fins.

symmetrical, as the top is usually only about an inch larger than the bottom. The caudal fin propels the shark forward when it's sprinting toward its prey.

ELECTRORECEPTION

In addition to hearing, seeing, touching, tasting, and smelling, all sharks have a special sense that humans will never experience: electroreception. Great whites have special cells in their snouts that allow them to sense electromagnetic fields. Under the Earth's surface, there are electric and magnetic currents that change according to location. This sense allows sharks to use electromagnetic waves as a road map. As the waves pulsate through the Earth's crust, great whites understand them and are able to use them to navigate during their long migrations.

LATERAL LINE

Found in all fish, the lateral line runs from a great white shark's head to its tail, down the side of its body. This line makes fish extremely sensitive to touch, in particular, to vibrations in the water. A great white is able to detect movement up to 820 ft. (7.3 m) away. The lateral line is so sensitive that when a great white detects movement from another animal, the shark knows the direction the other animal is traveling.

TEXT-DEPENDENT QUESTIONS:

1. How did the great white get its name?

2. Why is electroreception important for sharks?

3. What are the three methods great white sharks use to hunt?

RESEARCH PROJECT:

If great white sharks were to become extinct, how would that affect the ocean's ecosystem? What animals in particular would overpopulate? How would this affect coral and plant life?

WORDS TO UNDERSTAND:

cage diving: An activity in which marine biologists, scientists, and shark enthusiasts are lowered into the ocean in a secure steel cage, allowing them to have an up-close encounter with marine life.

chum: Shark bait consisting of blood, fish, and bone. The strong smell of chum tends to attract sharks.

decoy: A fake; something that is pretend.

CHAPTER 4

ENCOUNTERING A GREAT WHITE SHARK

Shark enthusiasts, marine biologists, surfers, scientists, and swimmers regularly put themselves near great white sharks, sometimes without realizing it. It's entirely possible that if you've been in the ocean, you've been near a great white shark and didn't even know it. Remember, a great white encounter can be scary, but rarely fatal.

Great white sharks could be nearby and you would never know it.

We often hear about attacks on surfers, and this makes sense. Although sharks have excellent eyesight, from the bottom of the ocean, a shark wouldn't be able to see the surfer—it would only be able to see the surfboard, which could easily be mistaken for a marine animal. Amazingly, Shannon Ainslie, a 15-year-old surfer from South Africa was attacked by not one, but two sharks, and lived to tell the tale. He was out surfing, and while riding a wave, a shark breached out of the wave and latched onto his body. After the shark bit him and pulled him underwater, he came eye to eye with the great white. Shannon said that the shark's mouth was wide open and he was able to see the shark's hundreds of teeth. The shark swam around Shannon, nudged him in the back, and then shockingly, swam away. Shannon was able to swim to shore and only suffered minor injuries.

Bethany Hamilton lost her arm in a shark attack. She is one of the most successful surfers in the world.

One of the most famous shark attack survival stories is that of Bethany Hamilton. When Bethany was 13 years old, she was surfing off the coast of Hawaii. She was taking a break from riding the waves by lying sideways on her surfboard when she felt something grasp her arm. She looked down and saw that her arm was being attacked—she never saw the shark coming. The shark tugged and tugged—eventually taking Bethany's arm. Bethany said that once the shark had a taste of her arm, it decided it didn't want any more and swam away. Bethany went on to become one of the most successful surfers in the world.

Tagging a shark with a tracking device can be a dangerous endeavor, as a shark's tail is extremely strong and can easily cause injury to anyone who gets too close.

WILL I GET ATTACKED BY A SHARK?

It's healthy to have a fear of dangerous animals—that fear is what keeps us safe from harm and lets us know when it's time to run away! That being said, it's very unlikely that you'll ever be attacked by a shark. Out of every million people in America, 1.6 will be attacked by a shark each year. You have a better chance of being struck by lightning (ninety-four people out of a million get struck each year)! If you find yourself in the incredibly unlikely situation that a shark would bite you, experts agree that the best thing you can do is fight! Sharks respect strength, and it's likely that a shark would let you go after biting you if it sees that you're not going down easily. Experts also agree that in the event that a shark actually approaches you in an aggressive way, punching the shark in the nose is the best way to surprise it and give yourself a chance to get away. The shark is likely to be so surprised that it'll be confused for a moment and forget what's going on.

That being said, remember it's extremely unlikely that you'll ever be a victim of a shark attack, even if you spend a lot of time in the ocean. The best thing that you can do for your own safety is to be aware of your surroundings, listen to lifeguards, and swim only in supervised areas. If you see a great white shark and the shark does not seem interested in you, yell, "SHARK" as loud as you can, and swim to shore. Remember, the shark has much more delicious things to eat than people!

Likelihood of Death from Certain Animal Bites

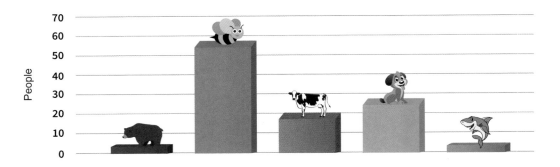

Surfers aren't the only ones who are in harm's way when it comes to sharks—even scientists trying to learn more about how to help sharks find themselves in dangerous situations. Tagging a shark with a tracking device can be a dangerous endeavor, as shark's tails are extremely strong and can easily cause injury to anyone who gets too close.

Now that you've learned quite a bit about great white sharks, it's likely that you'd love to see one in real life! Remember, great white sharks can only be seen in the wild, as they cannot survive in aquariums. There are a few different ways to encounter great white sharks if you'd like to see one up close.

Biologists sometimes use a wooden seal decoy to attract great whites to the water's surface.

Cage Diving

Cage diving is a unique way to get up close and personal with marine life. When you cage dive, you will be completely enclosed in a steel cage that sharks (and other animals) will be unable to penetrate. Your boat's captain will drive the boat to a location known for great whites and will then secure you (and a friend, if you like) in the steel cage. The boat's staff will give you specific instructions on how to act in the cage (keeping hands and feet inside the cage, not reaching out to touch the sharks), and it's very important to pay attention and ask questions if you feel confused. You'll be fitted with special equipment to help you breathe underwater (the equipment will differ depending on how deep into the water the cage will go). Your ship's captain will then lower the cage into the ocean, which will be attached to the boat with a steel chain. The ship's crew will throw some **chum** off the side of the boat (or drag a **decoy** behind the boat) to attract a great white, and with any luck, you'll get to look one of these amazing predators in the eye!

There are four places in the world where you can cage dive with great white sharks. The first is Seal Island in South Africa. As its name indicates, Seal Island is covered in the great white shark's favorite dinner. Cage diving is available at Seal Island from April to mid-September. Sharks are plentiful in South Africa, but the greenish ocean water can make it difficult to see underwater. Your next option is in Isla de Guadalupe, Mexico. The clear waters here can make it easier to see the great whites approaching from further away. The best time to see great whites in Mexico is from August to October. The Farallon Islands in California are another option to get up close and personal with great white sharks. The islands are 28 mi. (45 km) off the California coast and are loaded with elephant seals—perfect for attracting hungry sharks. The best time to see great whites at the Farallon Islands is from September to November. The Neptune Islands in South Australia also offer opportunities to cage dive with great whites. In the winter, the area is loaded with seals, and female great whites up to 20 ft. (6 m) long show up regularly to go hunting. South Australia is the only place in the world that will allow you to take a cage all the way to the bottom of the ocean to fully experience the world of a great white!

Cage diving is one way to see a shark in its own habitat.

Shark Watching

Does cage diving sound like it might be a little too intense for your liking? No worries—locations that offer cage diving also offer on-the-boat shark watching. Some shark enthusiasts feel that watching from the boat is even better than cage diving, as you're more likely to get the chance to see a shark breach as it attacks its prey.

You can shark watch from the safety of a boat.

LEARNING MORE

If you're not in a location where you're able to easily view great white sharks, there are still many ways to learn more!

Studying Marine Biology

No matter how old you are, it's never too early to begin preparing for a career as a marine biologist. Let your science teacher

Some malls display models of sharks for viewing.

know that you're interested in marine biology as a potential career, and ask for projects that will help you learn more about ocean life. Science and math are both very important when studying marine biology, and it's important that you keep your grades up so that you are able to pursue this career. Marine biologists are essential to the healthy survival of our oceans.

Attending Expert Talks

Call the biology department at your local college or university, and ask if they offer free lectures. You may be able to attend talks from expert oceanographers and marine biologists for free. This is a great way to learn more about great white sharks and other ocean life, even if you're not able to be there in person.

TEXT-DEPENDENT QUESTIONS:

1. What are the four locations in the world that offer cage diving?

2. How do boats attract great white sharks for cage divers?

3. Besides seeing a great white, what are other ways you can learn about sharks?

 RESEARCH PROJECT:

Some scientists leave the cage and actually go scuba diving with great white sharks. Research how scientists do this and stay safe.

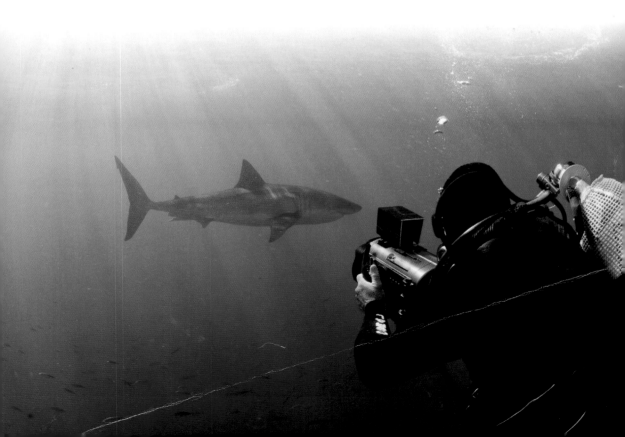

SERIES GLOSSARY OF KEY TERMS

Apparatus: A device or a collection of tools that are used for a specific purpose. A diving apparatus helps you breathe under water.

Barbaric: Something that is considered unrefined or uncivilized. The idea of killing sharks just for their fins can be seen as barbaric.

Buoyant: Having the ability to float. Not all sharks are buoyant. They need to swim to stay afloat.

Camouflage: To conceal or hide something. Sharks' coloring often helps camouflage them from their prey.

Chum: A collection of fish guts and fish remains thrown into the ocean to attract sharks. Divers will often use chum to help attract sharks.

Conservation: The act of preserving or keeping things safe. Conservation is important in keeping sharks and oceans safe from humans.

Decline: To slope down or to decrease in number. Shark populations are on the decline due to human activity.

Delicacy: Something, particularly something to eat, that is very special and rare. Shark fin soup is seen as a delicacy in some Asian countries, but it causes a decline in shark populations.

Expedition: A type of adventure that involves travel for a specific purpose. Traveling to a location specifically to see sharks would be considered an expedition.

Ferocious: Describes something that is mean, fierce, or extreme. Sharks often look ferocious because of their teeth and the way they attack their prey.

Finning: The act of cutting off the top (dorsal) fin of a shark specifically to sell for meat. Sharks cannot swim without all of their fins, so finning leads to a shark's death.

Frequent: To go somewhere often. Sharks tend to frequent places where there are lots of fish.

Ft.: An abbreviation for feet or foot, which is a unit of measurement. It is equal to 12 inches or about .3 meters.

Indigenous: Native to a place or region.

Intimidate: To scare or cause fear. Sharks can intimidate other fish and humans because of their fierce teeth.

Invincible: Unable to be beaten or killed. Sharks seem to be invincible, but some species are endangered.

KPH: An abbreviation for kilometers per hour, which is a metric unit of measurement for speed. One kilometer is equal to approximately .62 miles.

M: An abbreviation for meters, which is a metric unit of measurement for distance. One meter is equal to approximately 3.28 feet.

Mi.: An abbreviation for miles, which is a unit of measurement for distance. One mile is equal to approximately 1.61 kilometers.

Migrate: To move from one place to another. Sharks often migrate from cool to warm water for several different reasons.

MPH: An abbreviation for miles per hour, which is a unit of measurement for speed. One mile is equal to approximately 1.61 kilometers.

Phenomenon: Something that is unusual or amazing. Seeing sharks in the wild can be quite a phenomenon.

Prey: Animals that are hunted for food—either by humans or other animals. It can also mean the act of hunting.

Reputable: Something that is considered to be good or to have a good reputation. When diving with sharks, it is important to find a reputable company that has been in business for a long time.

Staple: Something that is important in a diet. Vegetables are staples in our diet, and fish is a staple in sharks' diets.

Strategy: A plan or method for achieving a goal. Different shark species have different hunting strategies.

Temperate: Something that is not too extreme such as water temperature. Temperate waters are not too cold or too hot.

Tentacles: Long arms on an animal that are used to move or sense objects. Octopi have tentacles that help them catch food.

Vulnerable: Something that is easily attacked. We don't think of sharks as being vulnerable, but they are when they're being hunted by humans.

INDEX

FURTHER READING

Casey, Susan. *The Devil's Teeth: A True Story of Obsession and Survival Among America's Great White Sharks.* New York City: Holt Publishing, 2006.

Civard-Racinais, Alexandreine. *Great White Shark: Myth and Reality.* Richmond Hill: Firefly, Inc., 2012.

Kathrein, Jonathan, & Kathrein, Margaret. *Surviving the Shark: How a Brutal Great White Attack Turned a Surfer into a Dedicated Defender of Sharks.* New York City: Skyhorse Publishing, 2015.

Roy, Katherine. *Neighborhood Sharks: Hunting with the Great Whites of California's Farallon Islands.* Cambridge: David Macaulay Studio, 2014. New York City: Skyhorse Publishing, 2015.

Siders, Shaene et al. *Discovery Channel's Great White Sharks.* Horsham: Zenescope. 2014.

INTERNET RESOURCES

http://www.nationalgeographic.com/animals/fish/g/great-white-shark/
The National Geographic great white shark site gives interesting shark facts, conservation status, and provides eye-catching images for the shark enthusiast.

http://cnso.nova.edu/sharktracking
The Guy Harvey Research Institute (GHRI) Shark Tracking partners with the Halmos College of Natural Sciences and Oceanography in tracking and recording shark activity. The GHRI dedicates its resources to the preservation of marine life, including sharks.

https://www.worldwildlife.org/species/great-white-shark
The World Wildlife Federation's site provides shark myths and facts, species information, and gives site visitors ways to donate to great white shark conservation efforts.

http://cnso.nova.edu
The Halmos College of Natural Sciences and Oceanography provides shark videos and shark activity maps.

http://www.conservation.org/Pages/default.aspx
Conservation International's site gives users information on a variety of vulnerable and endangered species, including the great white shark.

http://saveourseas.com
The Save Our Seas Foundation focuses their efforts on specifically saving sharks and rays. Their website includes shark facts, a newsletter, and details about how to help save sharks and rays

AT A GLANCE

SWIM DEPTH

200 ft.

Hammerhead Sharks
Length: 20 ft. (6.1 m)
Swim Depth: 262 ft. (80 m)
Lifespan: 20+ years

400 ft.

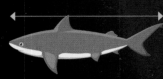

Bull Sharks
Length: 11.1 ft. (3.4 m)
Swim Depth: 492 ft. (150 m)
Lifespan: 18+ years

Rays
Length: 8.2 ft. (2.5 m)
Swim Depth: 656 ft. (200 m)
Lifespan: 30 years

600 ft.

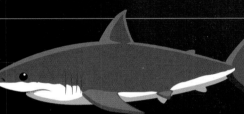

800 ft.

Great White Sharks
Length: 19.6 ft. (6 m)
Swim Depth: 820 ft. (250 m)
Lifespan: 30 years

Blue Sharks
Length: 12.5 ft. (3.8 m)
Swim Depth: 1,148 ft. (350 m)
Lifespan: 20 years

1,000 ft.

1,200 ft.

Tiger Sharks
Length: 11.5 ft. (3.5 m)
Swim Depth: 1148 ft. (350 m)
Lifespan: 50 years

Thresher Sharks
Length: 18.7 ft. (5.7 m)
Swim Depth: 1200 ft. (366 m)
Lifespan: 50 years

1,400 ft.

Mako Sharks
Length: 13.1 ft. (4 m)
Swim Depth: 1,640 ft. (500 m)
Lifespan: 32 years

1,600 ft.

1,800 ft.

Source: www.iucnredlist.org

PHOTO CREDITS

EDUCATIONAL VIDEO LINKS

Chapter 1:
Check out this video to see what it's like to come face to face with a great white shark!: http://x-qr.net/1Fs4

Chapter 2:
Get a shark's perspective of the ocean from this National Geographic video: http://x-qr.net/1FHb

Chapter 3:
Watch a seal take on a great white shark: http://x-qr.net/1HEH

Chapter 4:
Tagging a shark with a tracking device can be a dangerous endeavor: http://x-qr.net/1EWH

AUTHOR'S BIOGRAPHY

Elizabeth Roseborough is a former college, high school, and middle school biology instructor. When not visiting her favorite Caribbean islands, Elizabeth spends her time with her husband, son, and their fur babies, Titan and Stella, at their home in Dayton, Ohio.